SANDCASTLE EMPIRES:
ERODED BY THE TIDES OF ADVERSITY

Poetry by
David F. Kirk

Riverhaven Books

www.RiverhavenBooks.com

Sandcastle Empires is a work of the author's creation.
Any similarity regarding incidents is entirely coincidental.

Published in the United States by Riverhaven Books,
www.RiverhavenBooks.com

ISBN : 978-1-937588-58-8

Printed in the United States of America

Edited and designed by
Stephanie Lynn Blackman
Whitman, MA

Sandcastle Empires are grand in design,

but fragile in construction…

To my Mother and Father,

for their inspiration, support, and, above all, love

CONTENTS

THE SEASONAL ADJUSTMENTS

SPRING
The beating of wings, uninterrupted,
over the rooted, rotted maple tree.
Empty nests, as globed eggs spring
out into the blue-speckled afternoon.

You begin with wings and roots
and stumble upon independence.

SUMMER
The heating of bodies, forgetful,
on the sandy-blonde beaches.
Shadowed caves, as gulls dive
under the otherwise sunlit noon.

You have to be reminded of
the time when life was grand.

AUTUMN
The rising & falling of blood-red leaves,
like plots of empire, full of skulls & dust.
Swirling winds, unconquered conspiracies,
and the decline of vision for no good reason.

You are on the downside and
it cannot be ignored anymore.

WINTER
The trafficking in anonymous loss,
like bitter pills and swallowed regret.
The half-sweet streets are empty and
the night-forecast calls for collisions.

You wait on snow-white translations
but cannot avoid the hollow spaces.

CLAMORING

Wheelbarrows of words rusted out
from being acquainted with sadness.

The last call of an active-duty seagull.

A crab corpse kicked from behind
onto mountain clumps of seaweed.

The fall of sandcastle empires, unmatured.

An odd duck, with placid glaze, on disturbed waters,
in his own world, without the benefit of any drugs.

Who is watching over them?

An angel, you would hope,
over-protective custodian.

Unable to disarm Nature, it seems.

Watching the sea-swings of existence,
swells of euphoria & ebbs of cruelty.

Unscreened: has sunblock been applied from a Higher Power?

CREATING A NEW WORLD

Sand piles plotted
& a hawk spotted
on the retreat
from a pagan beach.

I believe in the other side,
despite lapses of concentration
& absentee devotion to
aisles of distracted thought.

A trial balloon for
the silver phantom,
who disappears into
the perfected sunset.

Sand and water,
muddied appearances,
and the exposure of
sun-tanned civility.

On a barely covered beach,
there's no pretense of
teasing out styled truths
in the stifling dead heat.

A STROLL FOR MEANING

I walk along a beach combing for meaning
to explain my place here, almost breaking.

I watch the waves crashing in "fear and trembling,"
and the unruly surges seem to overwhelm my being.

I am brother and son, both sinner and supplicant,
a man whose only exit is through seaweed & hate.

I should be seeing love,
but I am blind to it.

I should be feeling love,
but I am numb to it.

My mind drifts off to islands of escape;
I dread today, crowded with self-doubt.

Even as I dig my toes into the sand,
I can't forgive the shell I've become.

I hold on for reversals of fortune
like the horseshoe crab, stranded,

hoping for the coming of a high-tide,
to take him out again to secure waters.

I see the crab going out to sea and
am thankful for second chances.

The shot at miracles — staying afloat
as currents pull us toward redemption.

A SIGN OF HOPE

I come close to you with wide-eyed wonder,
like a child solving a puzzle with pieces missing.

I attempt to make the leap to integrate my soul,
despite the sharpened scissors of circumstance.

We all experience labor-pains,
mid-life crises, or "rotten luck."

Everyone tries to heal after
these cases of helplessness.

The progress isn't perfect
as we await interventions.

The Fall began with Adam and Eve
and the designs of our human desire.

The snake snarls at our outstretched arms
and then ambushes any claims to eternity.

Your people suffer terminal wounds and
surrender in make-shift hospitals of doubt.

Until you offer a gift to finish the puzzle
and an example to make complete the leap.

I will go on; I won't give up;
I will believe; I won't distress.

The heart will never stop beating.

HIDE AND SEEK

Light-green apples, bruised & scattered,
upon the ground recovering from frost.
The nip and thrust of a lost tranquility,
even the fraud at the core of my being.

I longed for labor in fertile front yards,
desperately dreaming of peace & quiet.

To hear the snap from the cold-blooded wind,
like a piercing whistle through a mouthpiece.
The shrill recorder of gray-swept episodes
or storms belonging outside of scrapbooks.

I mourn the lifting of the fig leaf,
discreetly in place all these years.

Abrupt shift to a state of nakedness
covered in the gold-flaked orchards.
The posing with smiles for the camera,
even as an illness takes over like winter.

I am with you, under the tree of ripened regret,
unable to focus upon the fruit that hasn't fallen.

If only I could grow with the hint of sweetness,
from a solitary seed to a shared taste of success

to work to prevent the rotting
in a vast cemetery of my mind.

I will not let my soul be buried; I will not wither;
I will rise from under the weight of circumstance.

AT THE CORE

The apple does not fall far from the tree:
you re-examine the gravity of the mind
as the immature fruit of thought ripens.

The bruises are noticed on the far side.

You slip and slide toward rotten luck,
as you toss aside a few bad apples.

The lingering in memory is
like a game of hide-and-seek,
which you never can win.

The players begin to battle for attention,

to rattle the senses and to shutter the blinds,
as you see past the sun in its own potency.

The coating of a plain vanilla cake
still comes at a cost down the road,
as the frosting on life is bittersweet.

The meeting-house is suited for good spirits.

To distinguish the wood from the rot —
secrets caught and relieved of counsel.

The victims are noted with full disclosure:
you oppose that which you will not deny,
as Evil is capitalized in small front-yards.

The apple is documented at rest,
in the fashion of a discreet Fall.

UNDER SUSPICION

The flattened demons, the smoked-out clouds
disappointing
in the direction of dead-locked experience.

I hear the voices; I hear the voices;
ill-tuned
like a guitar lacking the relevant string.

The inappropriate song, the whisper
devastating
like a compass of white-water regret.

I see through swollen eyes, vacant stares,
separated
like two isolated clumps of sea-grass.

The bittersweet opening to a better world
savoring
sunflowers growing old in middle-aged fields.

ENDANGERED

He belongs to the class of the forgotten:
clotted memories from a distant song,
like the combat-tested finch, at odds
with the empty-nested gods of eternity.

To let go of twenty years, overnight,
like winged regiments of specimens,
dismissed, courses of fast-acting flight.

Everything is up in the air.

The ones he knew so well
gather beneath the open sky and
close their ranks on Memorial Hill.

They recall together the peaks of autumn —
their cradled joy, and their tailored success.

He still chews on the seeds of remembrance,
feeding on feelings of what has been taken,
overheard from a bird sanctuary and
the fluttered thoughts of inexhaustible loss.

He is a stranger upon a remote stage.
At great heights, he might fly or fall.

A stiff wind upsets his trajectory, like birds
who are more than capable of soft landings
in safe places dedicated to connecting lives.

The man, darting in and out of consciousness,
goes airborne again and musters the courage
to create his own nest, to be happy once more.

DIMINISHED CAPACITY

To dump the framework for fame into a pile of autumn leaves,
as the sharp fork in the road takes you past flamed-out woods.

The maple is on fire, and no amount of effort can put it out:
first-responders are at risk, shouldering the back-up plans.

To be bold enough to pack the black moods into carry-on luggage,
as the path to success trails off with the flight of expedited hunger.

The harvest moon is rather agreeable, from its ridiculous height,
as you try to pick out an opportunity to lift off over a blazed Earth.

To birth the cosmic rift, divided & ambiguous:
on the advice of counsel, you decide to flee —

to flee from what only the condemned choose to conceal,
in a tailored suit that neatly disguises incoherent thoughts.

There is plenty of blame to go around: plain-vanilla invitations
and the vainly-stated chances to extinguish an inferno within.

An anguished chronicler is forever ill, smoking his fill,
as the nostalgic drip of memory is too much to accept.

A drastic reduction of expectations is in order,
this season of the indisputable, instigated Fall.

LABORING

The blushing flower mixes with the fallen weed.

Gardens and their guardians
arise from nothing. Wonder &
the origins of a delicate tulip.

Vulnerable.

A human being and the bridges of discontent,
unable to connect the thoughts, taking the leap
into a thick alphabet soup of scrambled letters.

We all have our secrets.

We are conflicted: to open ourselves up to the light
and face potential blindness by an external sun, or
to disclose our problems or to protect our privacy.

The revolutions of the mind are still turning
over in graveyards where we cannot avoid decay.

UNCOVERED

The mums are buried & you landscape hope,
as if you can get beyond the roots of despair.

Idealism & realism meet.

The voice takes forty-plus years
to compose itself for a line or two.

Dragons are dragged from under the bed.

The sword is acquainted with blood,
& the sheets bear witness to struggle.

Green like the ghost of spring.

The lapse of seasons, the growing of rainbows, &
a jack-o-lantern is resigned to being gutted again.

All souls are not treated equally.

The rain slips through your fingers &
you anticipate the revolution of thought.

Underneath the topsoil, the rot is in rebellion.

DIGGING UP THE PAST

The tombstone flag beats in the graveyard: guarded grandiosity, and
a conviction that all victimized souls will be permanently re-assigned.

To mime that which you cannot hear: the wolves apparently howl
and exercise the power to escape beyond skulls that cultivate loss.

The cross is worn on the neck; crack-ups are processed in ordinary time;
and, the witch handles the broom that gets her into a mischievous night.

To brief the ghosts of brothers & sisters, bristling with the gristle of fear:
the gap-toothed vampire pierces the skin, and the blood runs like a river.

The obvious is oblivious to the mess that mobs the haunted spirit,
spontaneous letting-go, and the fluid situation chained to the past.

A self-imposed imposter hoards the candy of a puffed-up life,
until he gets violently sick, in the aftermath of acute suffering.

To rest on his laurels, and to listen to the whisper-white moon,
he tunes out the medium, who thought she had the answers.

A dance is a dance, even in the tedium of a monstrous life,
where giant, non-compliant spiders scare the hell out of him.

To panic in the private graveyard, for poorly-celebrated years.

BURIED MATERIAL

A predisposition to apparitions
who occupy moon-drenched yards
and liberate dry-boned neighbors.

The moans of cold witnesses,
ankle-deep on snow-pattered grounds,
where two footprints lead to mortality.

A pear tree is free of sentimentality,
and the dogwood has lost its bark.

Pink-fleshed dreams exterminated
by the spray of existential neglect.

Analytical words portioned-off
from subdued contemplation.

Where do the head and heart meet
in the crowded property of thought?

A mourning dove murmurs something
about the second coming of a spring,
where the least sound awakens fear.

The undertaker's scrap-iron shovel,
digs into unlucky victims of age,
unable to resurrect final tragic acts.

Private plots of grief are like emptied-out pockets.

A WAKE

A caretaker arranges for the burial of Sanity.
Minds lowered to rest in antique-white wards,
where needle-thrusts achieve a Buddha-calm.

The staff laughs about patient self-awareness
as it checks every quarter-hour on the blood &
the pressured symptoms of checked-out minds.

Vacancies in rooms scrubbed clean of personality,
where blank faces cross into Emotion's morgue &
wait to be waked from a deep, blue-hazed slumber.

Awakened, like a pebble skipped across
the newly-rippled water of consciousness.

To yearn for Freedom, not the kind in textbooks,
but the sort you find in breathing in lilacs one day.

Far from the crypt of containment,
where people pass like sandpaper.

And, you feel the grit of being — exhumed from the dead.

VACANT STARES

The midnight ghosts from the West Coast deny the sunshine past, and
the night sky is haunted by a tombstone moon, overdosed on darkness.

The fleshed skeletons in the hall-closet are dragged, kicking & screaming,
into an emergency-room present, as shooting-stars are scared into silence.

The spider is scarred by the code-blue threat, an all-encompassing web,
and the associated wounds are frustrated by the restart of the madness.

The sadness, O the sadness, finds its way into the scrabbled night
where you have scribbled down the information without the insight.

Invisible & indivisible, a sinister thought arrives at another's doorstep,
where the peace that you sought lies buried in the cemetery on the hill.

The chains still cannot be seen, but they are heard,
and the rattle of memory forces you to the brink.

The dread slinks into your bones, and
you are unprepared for withdrawals.

The walking dead stare into the blank slate, with a blank look,
as bedsheets uncover a prayer that floats to a medium of hope.

The midnight ghosts aspire to unchain the past and
fly unencumbered into an ever-accepting sunshine,

where a wayward soul is determined to get its wings.

IN A BETTER PLACE

The affirmations & prayers that soothe the hurt, curtain-calls
from the curator who oversaw the filing in and out of memory.

I would give anything to have you back, with or without a police-escort,
and the high-drama of an enduring sweetheart love, still held in trust.

The breadth and depth of respect — the firmly-held accountability:
the Will is determined to fill the fountain with sweet white flowers.

I am at a distance, tending to my own herd of troubles,
sheepishly present, as the good Father watches over us.

The wine and the bread, the rituals that define you and me:
the recovery sought-after — a life without a "how-to" manual.

I follow in your footsteps, the waking & the breathing,
until the illness is like a footnote on a life far too brief.

The long and the short of it: a didactic turn of the Ideal,
and the give-and-take measures of a down-to-earth love.

I write to you a sincere letter of gratitude, angels in the wings,
as even the highest of kings endure the cursed slights of Fate.

The slated blessings you gave me, the mechanics of second chances,
and the labor that brought us into a world incapable of reproduction.

I am incurably hopeful that we will meet again!

BENT, NOT BROKEN

The chief reason to worry is the sorrow of loss:
raw wounds reflect the ancient throbbing
at the heart of a single-minded hindsight.

To mingle the stained-glass with the plastic:
the mimicking of the long-forgotten traffic
as laughter was silenced on cobbled streets.

To stumble on after-school programs, staffed with mercy.
Memory is swept clean; care is put back into care-givers;
and momentum shifts from the custodian to the cathedral.

The work is stirred in the aftermath of insight:
the bells chronicle the legitimate passing-over
on the pilgrim's itinerary, terminally cut short.

To shut down the courted relationship
that skipped a beat, skirmishes of grief
in the grip of an operation to remember.

The absolute is delicately related to the lost,
who challenge what they cannot comprehend:
another rendition of grace gratefully accepted.

The repetitions congregate in the tested faith,
robustly restored in the four corners of a life,
in which the stalled understand a final rescue.

MOVING ON

The progress of disclosures, pristine commitments to revelations:
I open the somber chambers of my mind, and that roar is primed,
like a lion, who climbs the steps to a mountain of stubborn troubles.

The truth is hard, and the path to the truth is harder: divulgences,
as eviction notices are given to those who can't stand it anymore.
I transform the tricks of Nature into a chemistry of a broken-brain.

The chain-smoking & the choking are from another's world
where you are roundly criticized for a self-medicated wonder.
I accept none of the credible attachments to the cleaner within.

The mess is getting bigger, I'm afraid. Reason is in the back-seat, and
the person behind the wheel is a stranger on the lone road to sanity.
I work the habits, grab the routines, until the breaking-point arrives.

It is close; it is very close. Most of my anxiety is centered
on the stranglehold of an untold anger in the closet.
I can't make sense anymore of the jumble of wild thoughts.

I ought to get out of the jungle and ignore the lion's roar.
The progression of disclosures goes sour, as does the whine
that barely is heard in the sober recesses of the hesitant mind.

The resident is driven to the perimeter of permissible behavior,
and the rage is exhaled in a texted dream for better tomorrows.
I am not up-to-date on the ambiguity of Fate, still in the works.

A moving van, though, is designed to transport the handicapped,
as the map to an improved place is scrutinized for coastal living
and the warm climate where Reason is given a chance to succeed.

The season is ripe for second chances and acceptable exposures.

SAVORING

What if today was your last day? To lay down in a field with lions,
to yield a crop of corn & tomatoes conceived at a vegetable stand.

To witness the birth of a national monument, Washington or Lincoln,
and to pay homage to the play at the feet of cherry-blossoms.

To travel far enough to realize that you love home:
reading and writing, like the odyssey of the mind.

To help an artist with arthritis who begs for the relief of chronic pain:
a believer hopes for a natural expression of another world.

To express the wish, to find the niche beyond red-shirted failure,
as the overtime clock winds down in a game that is in the blood.

To dwell with family, thick oaks of experience, a lump in each throat:
to rest on the back-porch with a patriot singing a country-song.

What if today was your last day? To hunger beyond the daily news,
beyond the empire of contested lands & red-hot construction plans,

the money and the power and the status: houses and boats and cars,
and the things that contribute to the downfall of an unconditional love.

To watch a dove in the burning red bush, and the rush of feeling,
even the healing that comes with comedy, a belly-ache laughter.

The rut is in the road, though, and the lions will not wait forever:
to cross the line, and to harvest affirmations always leading to you.

UNDERLYING REALITY

The creased faces pout at a Thanksgiving feast, the stuff of craziness,
and the phases of festive gatherings in which you put up with the turkey.

To work upon the path of a Hallmark insight, the heights of the holidays,
as the ones you love are falling apart at the seams, large-scale sadness.

The library is full of the history of loss, as is the attorney's office:
voices are heard in a vibrant tumult of Nature's season to give back.

I cannot take the yelling in my ears, even as no one is making a sound:
mixed messages are telling; gratitude is taken off the grid of acceptance.

The middle-ground is permissible for a compromise, the mounded lies,
and the accumulation of compassion that starts with the treetop angel.

To train your eyes upon the stars, intermediate-level prizes, and
the concessions to a mind that has tried its best to quell the beast.

The least of us are happy, at times, in the electric-blanket: blemishes,
and the reality that the cold has rolled into town, renewed resignation.

I register the season for what it is: razor-sharp interventions,
with the snow-like whiskers hiding a trace of cookie-crumbs.

The crooked ones always attempt to straighten up,
in the great unsolved mystery that we contemplate.

ABSENT-MINDED

To blank-out, to welcome
even the threat of thought.

Transmitters shut-down &
you feel so unconnected.

Sleep, the lotion of sleep,
on the dry skin of a mind
unable to think on its own.

Not a flake of thought, not an impulse,
not an urge, not a resistance to change,
only the horrible panic of nothingness.

The flat-lining of thought, the crisis —
the rear-view mirror totally obscured.

The inescapable breakdown, the calling out for help,
to cross borders from an accidental & complete void

to a recovery enabled under blankets of medications.
To warm up from a single inkling put-together
into an idea, until restored to the health of thought.

Not sure where you are going,
you desire to come back to joy,
transported again to a safe place,

calling, after all, upon the indispensable tow-truck of memory.

SURRENDER

The spectacle of losing your mind
round on carousels of irrationality,
riding up-and-down, so far down,
upon the saddle of an unstable horse.

To combat invasions of thought,
as if an outsider is at the reigns,
blinding & conquering Reason.

Overtaking back-channels of communication
with yourself, self-involved in stooped nights.

The white flag is flying.

The spectacle of losing your mind,
surrounded, compulsive cheeriness.
You spin out-of-control, dizzy lights,
overheard laughter & mass confusion.

Will it ever stop? Can you ever get off this ride?
To be overwhelmed by tear-stained revolutions
within yourself, a conveyor of homeless thoughts.

To need some peace and quiet from this detached reality —
to find yourself within reach of relief, with appeals to calm.

The merry-go-round is closed, though, until further notice.

MOVING PAST THE PAST

Excuses like hornets
sting indiscriminately.

I am charged with chagrin over
the expense of an expansive past.

I no longer can rest on my laurels
for the inevitability of day-breaks.

The weather is heavenly and
yet I am in a cloudy situation.

The rats & monkeys
can't see what I see.

Full-toothed dragons &
the court-jester — slain.

The thorns pricked before
the throne of imagination.

Royal courts, bloody nights, &
coronations alertly disguised.

The chemicals interact
like children on swings.

Stop-signs sing with dismay
at the funeral of continuity.

I have had enough of emptiness.

OUT OF THE BLUE

He is of the mind to rewind the tape of youth,
but the truth is — he keeps watching reruns of
a documented life almost past the stage of revision.

He features hope in his filmed project of survival:
like the full-time endeavors of a seagull and
his feathered shuttles to a sky above the sea.

A man does what he has to do, not to go under,
in the business of busying himself, like a clerk,
observant & faithful, about to drown in the details.

He notes well the anxiety at a coming high-tide,
a worry now to avoid sorrow later —
sandcastles accidentally destroyed.

On his beach, just within his reach,
a man luckily plucks a child from danger
and his recognizable powers are lauded.

The goddess of destiny is aggressively pursued
by someone previously in blank-faced obscurity,
forever changing the intricate calculus of value.

Human life and its occasional heroic gestures
worth so much more than petty theft or death,
with pretty views of sunsets on the South Shore.

It is enough; it is enough, on a sun-tanned journey —
to time-travel to possible scenes of happiness,
& the broad sweep of a story past sand dunes,

where he is accountable to himself in all his red-nosed glory.

LIFT-OFF

He routinely prepared macaroni and cheese
for supper, in his den of solitary confinement.
The TV played the news, stories of abductions,
baseball, curtain-calls, and the death of fashion.

He wore the Polo collared shirts,
the Gap blue-jeans gifted to him.
He lived in a few cluttered rooms, and
only the inherited dog didn't collect dust.

He read the Masters from his solid oak bookcase,
groaning under the weight of other people's words.
Tolstoy stood out like a friend, extending an umbrella
in a downpour, to warn against getting lost in the rain.

He had that scare with the prostate a few years back,
middle-aged antagonisms and the dissolution of time.
He never would recover from the one thing he most feared —
a permanent grounding of spirits, like planes too old to fly.

He could deal with his own departure,
opening the curtains wide to the sun &
noting that the darkness would arrive
as it had before, uncertain destinations.

He was sure the future would continue,
if only for those gentle souls he knew,
bravely facing the worst-case scenario —
scared passengers after rocky landings.

He looked to the Father and the Son,
the concentration of good will aboard,
and prayed that he too would be saved
from his narrow life spent on a runway.

COLLECTIONS

The knot is tied, and I cannot loosen the hold of love,
despite the homeless thoughts loitering in my mind.

I dwell upon the public benches within, preoccupied
with the parking of progress, the hoarding of sadness.

The past is cluttered with the relics of memory,
blank records & cold cases, after resolution.

Missing for twenty years, disappearing from the public eye,
I have been known to accumulate piles of bankrupt shadows.

The grating cadences of a long-lost paradise,
where I no longer possess comforts of home.

I have been dismissed, like that one last vagrant soul
who never returns the favor, pays back the kindness.

The knot is undone, and I resort to chasing ghosts,
who may not be recaptured in a self-serving world.

I track the unwanted souvenirs of loneliness.

FRAGILE ACQUAINTANCES

Walking on egg-shells, stressed,
afraid of saying the wrong thing.

The stroke unbalanced at four.

A trigger of illness,
tired of being used.

A madness, not seen as purple-hurt.

The invisible dilemma —
the stand of hypocrisy.

A hyena manages a smile.

Lining up the suspects, so ashamed,
on a charge of desertion from selves.

I claim to know you still.

But, then I'm all over-the-map,
not even knowing myself well.

The bones rattle in the hope chest.

MATTERS OF EXPOSURE

The skeletons in our closet
on a brisk Halloween night.

We bring them out into the open,
flattering an exposure to the cold.

I am frightened into confession
by the empty white-boned skull.

Twenty years of fiddling with words,
and I have made no one any better.

The sin of passivity, lacking
the passion to spar with life.

We draw our swords against Death,
who might put to rest our memories.

Do we remember through eternity
our triumphs and our pack of sins?

Or are our lives erased
like puffs of smoke?

The authentic scare of uncertainty,
striving to be one with the universe.

Are you kidding? One with the universe?
I barely can take out the trash on my own.

No treats this Halloween for this adult —
only the fear of skeletons yet to come.

SHARP-TONGUED

A slice of eggplant-regret, or
reticent chords, unpracticed.

Like the voices trying
to knife through neglect.

The hectic composure of images, unpoliced,
in lanes padded with refrains & double-takes.

A maple tree, de-barked like a pup,
the celibate stripped bearer of sound.

The tenor of speech & reproductions,
on the fringe of unrestrained thought.

Assertions or flirtations with big words,
like "coherency," in handcuffed truths.

A world subdued, at the risk of falling apart,
within earshot of services, attended together.

Like the voices trying
to knife through neglect.

The wounds apparently are capable of healing.

GOING UNDER

The textured poverty, incited windmills, and
instilled power in the context of deprivation.

The child sneaks rainbow sherbet
with oatmeal suppers on the stove.

To skim gruel from the dance,
only after the music has died.

Carnivals of sugar-stressed interventions.

A flurry of fast-acting grandiosity.

Farmhouses on a lake, cold-seated listings.

The bank holds title to the empty houses,
pardoned dreams with recessed lighting.

To relish the resilient strategies,
to stay afloat, while treading water.

The caretaker sleeps with both eyes open —
moneyed disdain, planted firmly & soundly.

The groundskeeper, gutters and shutters,
in a hurry to reach for the indebted stars.

Three-stories of a bubbled surround-wrap
that can't cushion the unceremonious fall.

The radicals and bureaucrats can't find
common ground in a rich man's world.

Unplanned hiccups & vengeful occupations.

MAKING ENDS MEET

The phonebook is out-of-date, the computer obsolete, &
I question the defeat of a game played twenty years ago.

Where did the expedition go wrong?

To look sheepishly past the fellow Walmart customers,
deferred compensation & layaways that can't be put off

any longer. The frozen pepperoni pizzas are a steal.

The real issue is how much I can afford: penny-candy
and the five-dollar bills that buy too much of the junk.

Pick-up trucks in the lot, filled up with pink-slime.

To climb the ladder, then to descend sloppily, until
a stop before a back-door without a proper greeting.

The rain-check is in effect.

The glove does not wear well, like the acquittal
in the court of public opinion, where onions weep.

I am in deep trouble.

The Mustang is on fire in the empty lot, polka-dotted calls,
emergencies, and the dispatcher can't afford to be wrong.

I put up with this crap & the tight-lipped indulgences.

The yellow smile weaves itself sick, prickly associates
on leave, under management working in the warehouse.

The society-mouse redecorates gossip beneath the fold.

UNSTABLE

To scan the barcode without you behind the register:
the red-line has been drawn & the retail sale is final.

A bomb is set to go off in the handicapped spring.

To adapt to the stop & start of rush-hour diplomacy,
where the traffic doesn't have a beginning or an end.

A hurried boredom builds up on the existential borders.

To send a message to those in the throes of crisis:
the status quo lands itself in a world with a jailer.

Bail is set forever at an astronomical price.

To gaze at the stars that dot the landscape of memory:
the bargain-hunting is forgotten in the sea-side shops.

A seagull is in the full service of a larger need.

To forge a relationship with those who will survive:
the target has been assigned, like cracked clam-shells.

A scavenger has its own vision of revenge.

To versify when the seats are losing their bearings:
a sabotage finds its way onto the negotiating table.

A man boasts of carrying a weapon of well-kept relevancy.

To choose the path that leads him away from temptation:
he returns to the blue-light special of miniature stressors.

A rocking cradle always comes with an untold cost.

IN YOUR CORNER

To abuse the word "marvelous" in a block-grant of ideas,
where a niche is carved out beyond monthly food stamps.

The camping on the front-steps of City Hall will do no good,
as the memory of an activist is looted from a trailer of time.

To petition for happiness, even in the frost-bite of comfort,
where a cold-remedy is swallowed in the interest of a cure.

The endurance of a grassroots elixir is tested anew,
as a selected few, the lucky ones, plot for a big day.

To stay the course is your only choice: to rally
around advocates of a hand-up, not a hand-out.

The bus that transports change is having trouble
within the bubble of busy bureaucrats in a polity,

a "silent majority," that hears what it wants to hear —
the preaching of civil servants, "not in my backyard."

To let down your guard, to push for the very poor,
even as efforts are instigated to crown the well-off.

The coronation of free will and the responsibility
to bolster a sense of reliance upon a regal thought —

Reason is my master, as rational economists claim
to be under its spell, under its rationale for service.

To learn that the budget never can be "marvelous" if
it includes cuts & slashes to programs for the people.

People, excluding & excluded, spar for a just outcome.

THE COST OF LIVING

The scope of discussion narrowed:
like the competitors in dodge-ball
weeded-out until only one survives.

The weather is kind of crappy,
snow showers & slick roads,
and it ain't getting any better.

The heating bills are through the roof;
the teeth aren't covered, nor the eyes.
Each month it's time to cough up cash
for insurance premiums, hot dogs, & drugs.

The cat is sick and the dog won't eat;
 it is hard to remember a "night out."
The waistline isn't getting slimmer,
& middle-age is fast approaching.

But, you know what? Even as
the world turns us inside out,
with its "arsenal of devastation,"
I am happy to be around — at all.

BALANCING ACT

To exercise upon the tight-rope, to walk the fine-line,
in the fight for compliance, in the flight from excuses.

A dying wish is to exorcise the demons,
that curse the core of the corrupted soul.

The back-room deals are smoked out;
the examinations are at cruising speed.

The results are posted, and the dreams are kidnapped
in the search for an appropriate contact to notify me.

The candles are lit in perfect rows
connected in an automated wonder.

To hide behind a veil, strings of mercy,
& the constant striving for forgiveness.

Evil works itself out, in role models of discipline,
as the disciples ramble through their own routines.

The tombs are guarded by enforcement teams;
excursions are planned with the habit to camp.

A gas-lamp illuminates the endangered spot
where a stone-hard fact is that I never will fly.

The last offer to buy my peculiar freedom
with the anticipation of a simmering hope.

Great expectations with poor realizations:
I never will rely upon gestures of charity,

for the safety net has come undone.

FILLING A VOID

Your plate is full. The push-and-pull of the frustrated lives,
where olives are emptied five years after an expiration date.

The dining room is crowded with things that crawl in the dark, and
you are rumored to fall into a place where the silver lining is faked.

Your plate is full. The yards are ripped out of the playbook of a hoarder,
and the scrap-iron mess ages before the eyes, wet with the sweat of denial.

The muffled-cry is erased from an all-out universe
where you haul out the trash & curse the still-night.

Your plate is full. The unforgettable sight of a small orange mitten
as you organize a domestic crusade brushing up against loneliness.

The bones in the back are retrieved by a Yorkshire terrier
who accents the influence of the forked road to normalcy.

Your plate is full. The door is open and the soap is in use:
you choose to embrace the caseworker's plan to improve.

The muse will appear, on its own time-table,
and the meaning of life will be condensed into a can,

until the chicken soup supports the process of healing.

STEP BACK, MOVE FORWARD

The proud are announced in a loud procession:
family lessons intervene like a cloud, dressed
in the pure buttermilk of an old-fashioned sky.

The black-and-white world is a throw-back
to a distant happiness greased with jukeboxes
in diners, where you always had enough to eat.

Evil did not have a home-town voice in a bipolar past,
where the curtain was drawn to minimize sadness, and
the blinds closed upon the Main Street preoccupations.

To lock away the nostalgia, in a rose-colored vault,
where faults are ignored, and even folly is tolerated,
like a missile crisis that almost put us out of business.

To return to the activated present, with credit cards overdue,
and Social Security and Medicare on the chopping-block,
with a safety net torn for those one accident away from doom.

The history of ours is full of plumes of smoke,
and the folks are always worried about the fire
and dire consequences for loved ones left behind.

The theft of memory remains, both the good & the bad,
as you steal away from the scene of the crime,
with the smoking-gun still in your petty hands.

To pander to a people, accustomed to piña coladas,
who serve out their time in restaurants and resorts,
where money contributes to a better way of living.

The gifts may not matter, unless you ask the debtor.

CHALLENGED

The deficit has us in a crisis, craftsmen all aboard, and
the oar-fish swims like an eel in dark and deep waters.

To finish the sworn testimony on a drawbridge,
which led from normalcy to a place of despair.

The mainland is loaded with modes of transportation
as the boats approach the vibrancy of the city's shores.

To close down, almost drowning under the pressure,
as the destitute are on streets, with apathy & atrophy.

The trophies are dusted for prints, half-lives after the fact,
as chemical agents tremble upon a landscape of collisions.

To scan the check-out counters for any sign of a pulse,
with a disintegration of the integration of the disabled.

The table is set, and the gray matter is compromised:
gratitude comes in many forms, and in many shapes.

To pour all your love into resurrecting the rivaled past:
the surplus goods are consumed with equal opportunity.

Equal partners arise from sky-line to ocean-front,
where the challenged still have something to add.

To order rounds and rounds of congratulations
with a declaration of dependence upon an Ideal.

Equality swims and flies with the best of us:
a bus is righted by the handicapped summer

in which you are at the pinnacle of accomplishment
and all the cliches go streaming out of the window.

UNDER-CURRENT

The pre-existing condition is not covered, over-the-edge,
and the hedge-funds are millions of miles away from you.

Mountains are made out of mole-hills, the lack of control,
and a daunting task is to awaken the sleeping giant in you.

The saints are on peace-keeping interventions in the mind,
as you are spared the flare-up of a regional conflict within.

The allegiances are to a world in which you vent and vent,
as the message sent is received with eventual equanimity.

The health predicament could not have been predicted,
and the head of the class now is bullied in the back-seat.

The lull in the action is like the protraction of the pain,
as you cannot enjoy a temporary vacation from illness.

To go completely quiet, then to dim the lights:
a seagull on the beach is in an ocean of trouble.

To be without insurance or the forms of treatment:
the departments of health do not work on Sundays.

The efforts to get better are continually being improved,
as even the bridge that links me to you is under repair.

The constant push & pull of an elementary Reason,
where you investigate the forces that drive us apart.

The investments have long since been made, and
the returns have left you with a challenged brain.

The fallacy is that the tension is too much to take.

ON THE RISE

The unequal distribution of wealth, the rocky seashores,
far from summer mansions & polished silver teaspoons.

A replica is made of a ship, sailing out of a harbor,
but the real deal lies outside of souvenir giftshops.

The main streets the tourists crave are paved with dollar signs,
as a man is released, without fanfare, from the overnight shift.

The work is sifted through an hourglass, minimum wages, and
sages are too smart to allow for summer vacations for the staff.

Any kind of travel is out-of-the-question, and
gravel-bed answers have to adapt to that end.

To help close the divide, to guide the poor to riches, and
to make a pitch for a core dignity after a hard day's work.

The surf & turf mentality and the send-offs in a world
in which the gap between the haves & have-nots exists

until they crash upon the rocky seashores, and
sleeping-giants awake from a pressured poverty.

The vessels are salvaged, on course to a wind-blown Equality,
even as a steering wheel is never fully under their control.

TAKING STOCK

The line between Good and Evil is drawn
where no one can be sure: the target moves
from warm-fronts to low-pressure systems,
where you pray to survive a blinding rainstorm.

A reservoir of good will is spotted from the shore,
where loons are said to swoon like lost love birds
who disappear into the heart of the distressed night.

The fight for romance, and the flight from chaos:
you order a life where trophies matter too much &
premiums are paid for success in a decadent world.

The gap of inequality between groups grows wider:
a bear emerges from a cave, a bull from a ring, and
they are charged with crimes in a competitive market.

The economy of compressed lives, flags regulated at half-mast,
as suits commit unspeakable acts, playing possum within sight,
as heated accusations are mounted & hard evidence is revived.

Opportunity has become pegged as a game where insiders,
the masquerading elite, hide behind the black-ink portfolios.
They manage to trade in stations powered by masked deceit.

The line between Good and Evil is drawn out
with invisible markers, where guilty consciences
conceal the various stages of bankrupt deals.

Wary of upper-echelon punishment,
we all are equal in trying to get away
with decisions & deeds we try to forget:
we let our suffering speak for our sins.

CHECKING OUT

The grit of intuition. I feel for you and those who rely upon halo-secrets.

To get by with your clouded vision under a sky-blue judgment,
where a flurry of blank checks are signed in advance of closing.

The looming cancellation of your line of credit, and
the reserved balance of over-the-counter disturbances.

To swear by the notes & pills, furiously clerked & deposited within,
as even the hoarder withdraws himself from the side of his disorder.

The bed is made again with a supervised memory:
he discards the folly of a safe past wasted in crisis.

To overlook the serpent, totally spent in the ancient spring,
as he calculates a meticulous present beyond any measure.

The treasure in the safe deposit box is locked, for now.

WEATHERING THE STORM

The lucky break isn't so lucky. It strains the consciousness and
severely hampers the glowing outlook that collapses in upon itself.

The volunteers panic within the constricted pathways, look-outs, and
the urgent call to attend to those who may lose what has not yet gone.

The upfront mission is all yours, with heads delegated in the clouds,
revising the numbers, and fidgeting the numb reality of invisible pain.

The vain attempts to advocate for a change, a radical change in thinking:
a lonely procession gets nothing from a process of admitted helplessness.

A wish is pretty well prone to tropical depressions of thought,
internalized trauma, practically bare cupboards & empty shelves.

A prayer is broken, like the bread in which you said you believed,
even in a rain-soaked aftermath of an unexpected tsunami of fear.

The Red Cross makes extravagant attempts to level the field
in which love & luck are handed out with unequal measures.

IN A DEEP FREEZE

The bones are chilled, and the bills are frozen
on a most depressing day I would rather forget.

To be in debt up to my eyeballs, war-chests, and
the bath taken on stocks in the emerging markets.

The splurge and the plunge in a polar vortex,
as gloves are poorly suited to badger the cold.

To thaw out the tempest, where guests saw work-boots,
and the smirk that wasted no time in polishing the face.

The small blades shield a crack in the temper
as a black-out cascades onto the trading-floor.

To float the rings from a petrified tongue,
and to blow smoke for broken resolutions.

The gusts of arrogance yellow on the eve of a reprieve,
when money mattered more hidden under the mattress.

To brush the teeth of a storm: sleeping giants and
greed that the lizard commandeered from a friend.

The green eyes penetrate the brisk grind of a target,
as snow papers proof that snoozed through the night.

To hibernate, so far from the deep pockets of a regime:
disturbances make amends, and redemptions go to rest.

The hiss of a guess is like a problem to be solved,
in the underlying tenor of terror, where a clock ticks,

as the bellicose warning clicks, for an unchosen tomorrow.

HANDICAPPED

The crutches splinter into a million pieces, and
the unspeakable is swallowed: too many pills.

A preferred sparrow waits, tufted wings, tinged with violet:
why? Why does the arrow strike without backup support?

The voice is speckled with honor, consumed by choices,
savoring and wavering in a meadow of chocolate daisies.

The line goes dead; the take-out order is arranged; and,
the close-up danger is in the dosing, long after the fact.

The intervening ghosts rattle the meek, with impeccable timing,
as the incremental push is to drive past the tainted woodshed.

The last-second cry of sheep faintly could be heard, and
the shepherd is shunned for not tending & inspecting fields.

A shield feels a little feeble, and the pebbles are too small:
I would do anything to ease the flanked appeal of a falcon.

To prey upon gentleness, with back-handed compliments, and
a prompt refusal to apologize in the nature of a profiled hero.

The prescriptions for individual courage are measured,
and group therapy acts something like a miracle-cure.

One final chance is to blend the personal and the public:
a blur of healthy check-ups & a scourge of unhappiness.

A hundred years of mixed reviews: empty refills
and the bottled sensitivity to a radicalized dawn.

LOST IN THE PROCESSING

The rose-colored glasses, irretrievable,
like data on the other side of normalcy.

What once was had, forgotten,
in the frozen ponds of thought.

Waiting for the coming of another spring,
like geese having dropped out-of-sight.

Do you know what it is
like to lose a compass?

To be without direction, or
the aid of past appointments?

The coming & going
of obliged visitations?

He can't make it on time,
and the payments are late.

The vase is cracked and
even the laughter is forced.

Back to the drawing board,
to slow the inner dialogue.

Hearing cycles of self-chatter,
he yields this peculiar harvest.

In the red-coated fields, ripe with conspiracies,
he covets acceptance from an unknown enemy.

SLIPPING AWAY

The shipping & handling of worry,
transported across open borders,
mindful of an infinite risk of loss.

A being without confidence after
exposure to one too many sunsets
in the double-vision of authenticity.

I cannot escape.

ON THE MEND

The bipolar world is approaching an end, parachutes,
and safe landings on the sandy beaches of normalcy.

A seagull has a damaged wing, overdue awakenings,
and the view from a day-room that doubled as a tomb.

I am better now, and the fog has lifted: from my window,
I spy an autumn bog with an embarrassment of cranberries.

To know enough to prove the doubters wrong, clouted doves,
who moved over the mowed-clover fields, fertile imaginations.

The bipolar world is tested by white-knuckled stress, fragile eggs,
and clear writing that enables me to present my best foot forward.

A nest is disturbed, and the little ones fly: a flurry of criticism,
and the direct assault upon the journey to a discernible Reason.

I am better now, and the fog has lifted: from my window,
I discover the sunbeam that seems to point to the rainbow.

A photographic-memory is triggered, beach-traffic, and
the epiphany that the broken ones have a shot at healing.

FLASHBACKS

A flurry of pictures scanned by
a man under internal demands,
where his lens is out of focus.

Institutional patient long past
the age of his coming of age.

Done in by wine-colored episodes.

Grasping for any exposure to Voice,
getting beyond a floor of negatives &
scuffling in dark rooms of thought.

Photographs of skeletons,
scraped of layered identity.

The appearance of bone.

In a corner, Reason, straight-jacketed,
unable to break free and improvise
in a domain of regimented impulses.

Blank stares, pill-boxes, &
clamped-down responses.

And yet never to bury the dream of a developed life.

NO LONGER NEEDED

The good you have done shouldn't be swept under the rug,
forgotten, in a world of multi-tasking and incessant texting.

The complaints are registered in delicate sites,
like the hutch that holds Grandma's figurines.

To tip-toe through a house, with day-to-day grieving,
where you suspend the belief in the company of love.

The recovery is privately doubted, but
you put up a front that it will work out.

Seizures and open-ended interrogations:
the delays in communication are hurtful.

Your heart, damaged in a black-and-white world,
will not collapse under the weight of gray-matter.

The brain does its best, beset by familiar trends,
like the dark aptitude to accept the unacceptable.

The dull obligation & the mask of politeness sit,
as the old reality sinks into a muddied grave.

To live & to give life: a voice that feels the pain.

You are better than good: the lavish gifts of love,
and yet destined never to get the thoughtfulness in return.

The bargains, swamped in the emotional discourse,
are kept in the closet, without even a bit of self-pity.

The internal bleeding goes on out of sight.

LEFT OUT IN THE COLD

A mind like a skunk, disgruntled,
prowling in the weeds of thought.

It threatens to spray an unsuspecting world —
the crimes of instinct on cold-hearted nights.

An outcast, governed by fear,
resigned to the dark shadows.

Blackened and rabid thoughts,
without a spotlight of Reason.

No stopping the associations,
no relief in sight, I'm afraid.

The awful smell of worry &
the desperate need for help.

A mind, like that rabid skunk,
attempting to adapt to disease.

Too disturbed to protect itself &
too isolated for Nature's interventions.

The grass is dead, and the weeds thick;
nobody told me that life would be fair.

AT A LOSS

The one that you love is in need of supervision:
he can't recuperate from what is hard to watch.

The head-on collisions with a stubborn hub of an illness, and
the botched attempts to recover without admissions of pride.

The confessional is ready to receive its first guest,
who is wrapped up in the tinfoil of self-interest.

To remove the loyal subject from the heat & lies,
as he rolls the dice again, playing against the odds.

A day that was craved has come to pass,
and you see the hounds released, at last.

The impulse control is shot to hell, and
you pray for a few good moments of peace.

The saving is done outside the purview of our Chance,
where fancy words for God's grace are learned by heart.

The burns are second-degree issues, where you use
a thousand points of light to illuminate compassion.

All that you give is left behind, as the hurdles are jumped,
and you fume over the mortal stake you put in the ground.

The frappes no longer satisfy, nor do the chicken-wraps,
that are like a drive-thru of culinary stop-gap measures.

The appetite has been whetted and
the can kicked down the road.

For today, the wind is at our back.

MISSING OUT

To remember your voice, the boisterous song and the ballad,
even the nursery rhymes that twinkled in your forever-eyes.

The lavender scent of the garden will not leave me alone, and
the pumpkin bread we shared was fresh, always just right.

To cherish the best that you put in to the mix, the whipped-up batter,
and the chatter about nothing in particular, except for politics & God.

To finish the sentences, and then to connect the thoughts,
you would do anything for anyone in the burnt-out woods.

The news was too tragic, and the mistakes too sad —
you blanketed the children and shielded their eyes.

To absorb the absolute strength of your love, like a feeling,
only "on steroids," in the best sense of our troubled world.

The desire to keep you with us, search-engines & scrambled-eggs,
and the lost ability to seek out what cannot be made whole again.

The pitter-patter of little feet, still growing up, and still filling out,
always with you, even after campfires & the smoke of tomorrow.

The promise to meet up again after the quagmire of missing you:
the hard-pressed butterfly will always reside in our broken hearts.

We don't want to let you go, but we will be reunited,
and your voice, your spirit, and especially your love —

will stay with us in solid-gold memory, until then…

PREVIOUSLY ENGAGED

The white-out of adolescent smiles, bracing
for another absent-minded crunch of snow.

An avalanche of pressure, bearing down on them,
avidly avoiding other sessions of man-made grief.

To become that which you cannot deny.

The hair-line fracture of Youth, breaking
a renegade man in his smoke-cloud pain.

An obsessive quest, recapturing ruptured dreams,
and putting together a reputation staked on safety.

To stand up to that which angers the soul.

The spirited exchange — both the giving & taking,
waiting on the sidelines for the other shoe to drop.

An anatomy of isolated requests, the worn-down livers,
drowning in a sea of whiskey-sours on saturated nights.

To be overcome by the past.

The ignited rings of fire & the ambitious bursts of air
stilled, stunted, even trashed in the frosted groves.

A minimal yield of oranges, bottled optimism,
harvested precedents, and thawed-out progress.

To support you, my love, unwilling to expire.

SANDY

To hold your hand all the while, during a sold-out performance,
before the last grandstand for the crowd on the boardwalk.

Loudspeakers squeeze out a haunted anthem,
like a phantom, who pleases the opera house.

To notice a sudden change in scenery, to charge up the batteries,
in the mean-streaked streets, where once-welcomed waters overflow.

The cold is coming sooner
than I ever thought it could.

The sincere goodbye is brought up, with the fear of one last supper,
steak & potatoes, as your appetite for living is too great to be faked.

To adapt to the rule-breaking insight: you will not fool around
with the devastation that leveled and shattered so many lives.

The antique platter, upon which your food rests, grows old, too,
like frosted flowers, as the hour of equality calls you homeward.

The beachcomber may find in time whatever
has been lost in the perfect storm.

Even the sailor gains the weight of worry
as the harbormaster is fed up with the loss.

Almost all of us have settled back into our usual routines:
the unseen mess of hard-core truths has yet to be cleared.

A final request is for the tall pine trees to stay standing,
to preserve the good Nature from a fall of life and limb.

The hymns that we used to sing are registered anew.

A SENSE OF EXTREMES

To transmit crimson kisses by way of swelled lips:
to lay on a beach, glistening with Coppertone sweat.

The heat is barely tolerable; the riptides are incredibly strong:
to separate fear from false-alarms, the actual from the artificial.

A fish, of no particular denomination,
never knows the pleasure of vacation.

To be sure of nothing but the vows that
follow from the vast output of the sea.

The senses are divorced from the dense knowledge:
to put stock in the reconciliation of work and play.

The day has dawned; the haunting has been reckoned:
a turtle, equipped to cope, creeps ashore toward safety.

The high-noon meal of ground-chuck & shoestring fries
never is intended to be a lasting prize for a hungry soul.

To swallow whole the theory of natural selection,
as evolving species revolve slowly out of favor.

The bottlenose dolphin surprises the world
with a fitness that borders on an adapted joy.

The unalloyed feelings and effusive emotions
fly in the face of dead-panned logic, flat reality.

Our authentic selves contemplate a June sunset,
so far from a reduction into elements of theory.

The weary wonder of spotting the belly of a killer whale.

A HAND UP

To flounder on the open seas, the flow of vacillations,
and the diligent application of regulations to the work.

I beg your pardon: the fish are not cooperating, and
your livelihood is on the hook for a spoiled lifetime.

The oil spill has siphoned off the best of the catch,
as loyal attendants persevere in hospitable memory.

Homeless, homeless, the rest of us are homeless:
the gulf between rich & poor is pooling in shifts.

To lift you up, coleslaw and a piece of fish,
under the sheltered laws of human kindness.

I wish I could expose the blindness, heavy-handed,
as the leverage is lost in the hesitation without sight.

The bait is in the water, still waiting for a taker,
as you give all you have to get through the day.

To struggle to live, to raise a family, always with tears,
with a resolution that a boat won't sink on your watch.

I won't be overcome by waves of apathetic reviews,
even as the path is disabused of the notion of love.

A community is in motion, summoning a spirit
that hears the muffled sounds of certain distress.

WAVERING TOLERANCE

The heated swells — that overwhelm the waking — anticipate a victim:
you trick yourself into believing in the controlled fever of the surf.

The hot topic in the tropics is the sanctity of the mission:
you are prompted by the first-sight of a mythical mermaid.

The sea creatures are sounding the alarm, murmurs of distress:
you swim through the waves on obsessed trips, time after time.

The lips are firmly sealed; the whales are breaching the surface;
you will try anything to survive the epic dimension of the surge.

The sand in your hazel eyes evokes unparalleled pain:
you say just enough to temper the storm raging within.

The earthly mistake is accepted in the spirit of forgiveness:
you advance a plan to revive unconscious urges to explore.

And hesitation gets you nowhere, blackened moods:
you go down gasping for the delicate necessity of life.

An unfulfilled life, zapped of energy, depleted of dreams:
you nap without certainty in the unmapped territory,

where you pray one day to wake up
to an uneventful day at the beach.

CRATERED ENTHUSIASM

To pocket the coconut in a milk-bath of tropical adventure:
the stature of a travel-goddess is assessed on gravel tracks.
Ash is everywhere, a stash of regret, and a cautious reverie.

The chivalry of a cause, and a rebellion against a volcano,
who calls out the tangerine sky, with blanket forgiveness,
and forgets what has passed in extinct tours of yesterday.

A texture of grit fits nicely into the barren theme:
teams of green-eyed spies attend to the astral dust,
as you grasp the gray that takes over absent groves.

There, nothing grows, and no one knows,
in the suffocating heat that turns itself off,
as the hard edges of suffering are softened.

I pledge allegiance to apprentice the moon.

THE INNER SANCTUM

The following is undecided:
bellows, incinerated pillows, &
the dinosaurs chain-smoking.

The stroke of luck & the loss
that comes with the territory.

The black-shingled repose, stunted growth,
evasions, and invasions of a private space.

Answers fall from the sky
& catch fire upon re-entry.
The cremation of thought.

Sought & dismissed, like so many souls,
like so many attempts at reconstruction.

The period is covered with shame
& you cannot help but question.

The test of patience, reliving
spots thought too hot to touch,
where your Self is up-for-grabs.

Keeping tabs on uncertain judgments &
unverified qualifications to condemn.

UNPROTECTED

I sleep while the sheep cry out
for observed pasture-violations.

The close-knit hill community wakes
to hear the deafening loss of kindness.

Foul weather unexpected, gray snow fallen,
blanketing this black earth with insecurity.

Sparrows locked in skies look down
from borrowed thrones, still aloft.

The lifting staff of shepherds, rebuked
for failing to exercise local authority.

Delegations of sheep, obviously moved,
known to sleep now with their eyes open.

AT ODDS

The black sheep grazes in the blank verse meadows,
where red-eyed demons ride seamlessly into the night.

The right thing to do is to acknowledge the shepherd,
who apparently demonstrates a home-field advantage.

To bandage up the wounds, under a full moon,
where the leader and his flock are out of sync.

To concentrate on the weakest link, and make it strong,
among the Good & Evil stew in the cauldron of conflict.

The odd conjuror has a magic potion to put you at ease,
like the poem, uniquely staffed, under another's control.

The present tense, and the pretense, of our creation remains
in the hands of someone totally out of our frame of reference.

To defer to his judgment, and yet, to exercise discretion,
in a closely-watched pasture, in a patch of shade & light.

RECTIFYING ABUSES

The rage in the eyes,
the black-afflictions.

Angel-dust & poisons.
An unlikely celebrant.

Split into factions:
to defend or deny.

Grown men, as ladybugs,
incensed at being trapped.

The just stakeout &
the red-hot bellows.

Crisis. Reversals and
an unpleasant fortune.

The broom sweeps
the mess that is left.

The Latin stands for housecleaning.

And I cry out Amen!

POSITIVELY TROUBLED

Virtue will not bend broken commandments —
like the promise always to honor your God.

Where did you go wrong?

A single glass-eyed toad
cleared out after the storm.

Could you not have done better?

A run-in with a posse of lizards
at daybreak on All Souls' Day.

Why did you fail?

On any other trespassed morning
armadillos act as armored guards.

What can you say in your defense?

The memory of close regiments
& distant bayonet-slips of light.

How can you be so far removed?

The snap of irrationality (my only excuse!)
in an insane world spilling blood in His name.

No more room for questionable conduct.

KEPT IN THE DARK

I wake up to the dream of better tomorrows,
after the alarm bells ring in the black-eyed night.

I unwind Time, as if it would never run out,
forgetting to attend to the beat of my stress.

I pledge to redeem myself in front of a crowd,
an audience so full of unprotected hearts.

I yearn to connect, beyond the confessional,
emerging from the box with unearthed intentions.

I am refreshed enough to share the buried gifts,
and I take-off with the coming of the hummingbird.

I had been trapped beneath the weight of borrowed words
but now am free to pursue the heights of pillowed skies.

A sunrise, unburdened with thoughts of completion.

UPSIDE DOWN, INSIDE OUT

To dredge up what you most dread: the furious gaze visited upon
a ledge, unstable recollections: silt slips through outstretched hands.

To observe the treacherous passing, masses of discontent,
outside the realm of manicured grounds and clean spirits.

Yards of pure & rich loam cannot cover up the clover of mistakes;
dead grass is weeded out on over-rated or under-appreciated lawns.

To prioritize and to reorganize in the warm surge of the spring:
split-second changes manage to unhinge the cold hold of thought.

To infiltrate the instant feeling of something deeply lost:
uninsurable costs and dented love, unable to be repaired.

Unfairness makes Inconvenience seem so small. A swift fall
for orange jumpsuits & the measure of unredeemed dreams.

To seem as if you are unaware (then aware) of the incident that
could rip the heart out of normalcy & kill your version of the present.

To learn acute lessons of suffering, crying on shoulders,
buffered by the belief in a world better suited for caring.

We all have our own demons in the central-booking of injustice,
places where angels are reluctant to wander, frightened to tread.

To arrive at human complicity in crimes against other creatures:
damage & denial done to those who share an instinct to survive.

To process the range of realities, settled behind white picket fences,
where we take issue with our own proximity to the next catastrophe.

Our concerns are taken down: rehabilitations rest beyond our control.

REFORM

The narrow escape from self-involved sorrow:
to concentrate deeply upon another's aspirations,
no longer stuck in the pose in front of the mirror
watching only the reflection of shallow self-interest.

The routinely-dismissed case of destiny:
blindspots, the sport of getting by okay
as you get more than you bargained for
as consideration of fractured community.

The skill within the skull to manage chaos:
like the cavemen who first created art
upon the walls of dwellings
as they aped what they saw.

The havoc of imagination:
the conscious attempt to imitate,
the competitive impulse to master, &
the well-traveled tradition to ascend.

The unplanned trajectory of flight:
freed from barbed-wire surrounding
a self-imposed prison, where many
serve out an inescapable sentence of

life without parole.

SENTENCED

The threshold to institutional commitment,
stages of alcoholic-obsessed vacancies.

No one is at home.

The warden is gone.

You are on the cell-block fleeing
from prescribed forms of restraint.

An apparition of normalcy,
a library, an exercise-room,
a "defense" against rioting.

The perimeter is secure.

The inner boundaries are insecure.

A resident acts out of frustration,
from his own inner, cluttered world
where birds are words of conspiracy.

What did he do to deserve this?

What can he do to escape this sentence?

Haunted by the thought, he will
never be free from this tyranny.

The bewildered face or facade of containment,
where you never know if you will be released.

ROLE-REVERSALS

The addicted are admonished for what they try to buy or sell:
money goes up in smoke, the tale of a role-model gone wrong.

The nonsense that you speak— indictments of moths
and the fraud of mosquitoes politely asking for blood.

Your mind is basking in the faded glory of trophy-rooms
where you prepare to enter a house of delayed meaning.

You resort to leaning on what no longer can be supportive,
in courts, as aggravated assault is in the character of calm.

A slip of the tongue cannot always be monitored,
the ankle-bracelet is removed, after house arrest.

The domestic charges are dropped,
with a slap on the wrist, dismissed.

To be free, finally, to state your case in a wide-open forum:
the pious & the unprotected are capable of switching places.

The "silent majority," the rank & file, are vulnerable
to frank admissions of guilt, to moments of weakness.

Temptations divide a harmonious home-front.

ON THE FRINGE

The loose-ends are gathered, patches of ash,
as choices are sensitive to the shiver of light.

The ice-cold coffee & the bones in the coffin rest,
as sold-out coughing fits are thrown under the bus.

The usual suspects thunder a drop-dead enthusiasm,
as dread spreads to other parts of spark-plug Empire.

The drugs hustled on the street always need a buyer,
as a fire warms fresh warnings on the gambled strip.

Impressions of frozen composure melt with the passing,
as one sculpted thumb signals another hitch-hiked day.

The excluded are omitted from the mainstream cathedral,
as drafts of a relevant history are updated on the margins.

Out-of-sight, the doubts haunt the grandmother's attic.

CUSHIONED EFFECT

An aptitude to surrender is planted in the self-absorbed night,
where you know that the critical thinking has to do with you.

The travesty of the grapes becomes the majesty of the wines,
as you tip-toe through the checklist of incumbent vineyards.

It depends upon the hint of grated interest, pressure-cookers,
and the immediate need for a drink to settle the frayed nerves.

You are willing to stay home, to incorporate depressions & flights,
into a therapeutic safe-spot where self-medication is done too often.

An intervention is in the cards: shrinking violets are disposed,
and the violence is the link to a temper that just won't quit.

The ridiculous and the unreasonable, in a group-meeting of experience,
where you are stationed with your own sponsored revelation of trauma.

You intend to make a break with the format of a shallow past,
as best wishes & condolences lead to the structure of a pillow.

A jury of peers is reluctant to cast a verdict:
the commands come from your inner voice.

The messenger is anxious to institute change.

AN ONGOING BATTLE

To walk the straight and narrow path from the stairs to the fresh-air:
the in-house temperament is rarely as hot as the temperature outside,
outside the scope of bone-marrow privileges, and the hurtful ordeals.

To be someone, still working himself up into a frenzy,
after a cacophony of mistakes, after the phony-disguises,
in a high-volume sweepstakes that he may or may not win.

To introduce himself to the gin & tonics, a bittersweet taste,
and his voice is heard in the aftermath of a siege of regrets,
in which he negotiates a truce with the bottled temptations.

To make his own news, with headlines of a strong constitution,
where amendments are internalized in the shelter from a storm.
Never to mind, never to succumb again, in the retreat to peace,

where the days are numbered, and
affirmations are determined, as he goes.

CROSSINGS

The final push into blushing night —
sirens strike a discomforting chord,
disconnected from un-affected bliss.

We all are reported to rush, fully stressed,
to the familiar beat of half-disturbed streets,
and the failings of our less-restricted selves.

To make an overture toward Happiness,
to overcome the darkened hands of Fate —
gray-bearded ghosts roaming in the attic.

The dismissal and acceptance of hymns —
recognizable (if not pure) sounds of love,
like suppers digestible, flavored with grace.

We all begin at the end of wit,
as chipped-toothed survivors,
grasping a note beyond reach.

To demonstrate beyond these boundaries,
to make our mark beyond ordinary limits —
clouds without the tyranny of interpretation.

The trying of our impermissible thoughts,
the crime of aging, the scars of dreaming —
as we march to scarcely-audible farewells.

These ill-placed hours —
retreating sadly & swiftly,
deposited on the other side,

after long-lasting impressions of safety.

ENVELOPING THE PAST

To tip-toe slowly through a tight-lipped past,
where no one replicates the weakened sound
that taunts Eternity out on any weekend pass.

The haunted clarify the dignity of forever sleep,
as they harass those with no business to dream:
ball-&-chains are deemed to justify the charade.

Dry eyes surprise the air-traffic controllers,
as the ghosts fly in patterns, lit by lanterns,
removed from the candlesticks of yesterday.

To chase the boom and bust heartache
that he keeps to himself, runway tirades,
and a drone couldn't find its way home.

One last stand, creaking premises, and
an oak-floor always supporting Hope —
written flawlessly in permanent marker.

A park bench is the site for Memory,
and the romance that flagged the mist
in the rags-to-riches story of feelings.

Feelings are said to survive, if only,
if only the flat-lined spirits rise up
with the steel-spine of commitment.

The prayer is spent on what cannot be spared
in the campus of contagious living and dying
as he out-grows the lamp that gives him light.

A brighter star is loaded with consequences and
honors the special needs that supplement a Trust,
that recovers to protect all the assets of true love.

BEYOND THE GRASP

The blinking green light across the shore,
the lipstick-red & rich lavender fireworks,
a riot of colors through country-club nights.

She brought up Gatsby & the wealth of desire,
unloading her feelings like a packed suitcase
from which came the clothing of authenticity.

She meant the world to him, and
he banked on a dream of true love.

They would become One, happy returns
after investments into funds of mutuality.

He never thought of going under or
submitting to depressions of thought.

Then she disappeared out of his life;
he was stung by yellow-jacket regret,
and the swelling went on indefinitely.

Such revelations are judged
to be too personal, I'm afraid.

The open market of romance:
the hidden costs of volatility.

DRIFTING APART

A pair of swans dared to separate in the bonded harbor,
where there was no daylight between viewer & subject.

To detect a mastery of craft, like the old man
who boldly returned the small bass to the sea.

A beachball is suspended in air, burgers from the Lobster Hut,
and the incongruity of waiting for something that won't come.

The fumbled opportunity to save the row of rowboats,
as the unnoticed leak in one gets progressively worse.

To float the idea that you will be in charge, salty language,
as you don't give a damn what others may say or think.

The family of seagulls has no bearing on the outcome,
as you see the individual boat sinking in raw memory.

To resurface and to cough up the waters of an amicable past,
where you are sure that the capacity for change has been met.

The perception that we share is that the old force of Destiny
pulls me to you, like a magnet, in its ever-divine bag of tricks.

The magic of Nature is within the context of an ocean of laws,
attracted by the cause & effect of what you cannot overcome.

To throw up your hands and to drink the rum and Cokes
that soothe a rattled brain which tries to order the open-seas.

The two swans make sense in their own little niche,
as Reason and Emotion are hitched for a purpose.

The marriage, though, is on the rocks.

PAIRED-UP

The anguish is disguised under the pear tree,
where a pre-nup has been declared invalid &
the couple's problems seem so insignificant.

You are matched forever with two issues: compliance & compromise,
where the meds for moods and thoughts are taken, one-by-one, until
the arguments are forgotten, back-and-forth, in the froth of a meanness.

To walk back from the mini-inferno of anger, fire-alarms,
where the head keeps itself from banging against the wall,
as love is tossed in the general direction of one's partner.

We will make it work, through the slog & murk of Fate,
until we unclog our brains from the tragic consequences
with good luck & belly-laughs and without provocations.

And the guests who never stopped coming arrive,
creating essential patterns on the back-lawn.

A plain-white cake is tasted, with its meaning tested,
but the mess that you created is almost all cleaned-up.

The positive relationship, stripped to its very essence,
bares the facts and restores its luster to a fulfilled life.

To trust in the basic functions of a vital existence,
with the good ends of compliance & compromise,
beyond bells & whistles, beyond the fancy rhetoric.

The ripened fruit falls from the pear tree,
and it leaves behind the blemished mark,
and the shadow, still born in the morning.

IN OPPOSITION

The petty-green majesties of flight, misguided,
like a missile on its course to violate the sky.

I hear you & cannot reach you.

The entire empire of my mind, toppled,
like a giant falling victim to compliance.

I am divided & cannot stand the pressure.

The civil war is raging, internalized still,
like cake after the candles are blown out.

I seek to redeem & refuse to scream.

The archives are irrelevant, dust-mites,
like liberators who arrive way too late.

I see a light & confuse it for success.

The safety-helmet is secure, risk-taking done,
like a man with a raincoat only after the rain.

I am so far from you.

ALL THE RAGE

Ancient spirits, sent back on fact-finding missions
in order to further the cause of liberty, repossessed.

There can be no justice in following
mammoth words with small actions.

As an aristocratic house is ravaged by rioters,
average colonists wake up to the ruins of relics.

The cabinet-maker is tired of closed doors, and
the silversmith provides the metal of resistance.

To watch the brilliant kite, painted with plain wonder, escape
into the heavens outside the scope of red-coated superiority.

The queue has formed; the judgment is about to be rendered.
It all falls upon the rage of rebellion, bells ringing clearly.

They hear the impulse to be strong
enough to deposit tea in the sea.

The origins of revolt, with disparate faces and places,
based in North America, struggling for independence.

Unwilling to mend fences or play games
in a heated atmosphere of duels & danger.

The stranger is feared to be next-door,
and the trespassing moment trembles in doubt.

The spirits believe forever in something
that cannot be seen or touched.

DAVID F. KIRK

THE BURDENS OF REVOLUTIONARY AMERICA

The precise cause of American liberty is a mystery.

The lanterns illuminate the shadows of sorrow,
upon an essential ride that never was inevitable.

The earth shook with the tremors of change.

The texts & tests of a revolting past exist
within the context of conflicted loyalists.

The learning & the slow-burning of effigies in the streets.

The hard dichotomy is between the head and the heart,
as they meet within the intersection of interest & ideal.

The real issue is the soft tissue of dissent.

The printer is out of paper; the apprentice has disappeared;
and the process of persuasion moves on without a master.

Common sense is the commitment to public esteem.

The reputation is sealed at the origins of healing, where
the unification of a campaign is said to honor the states.

The champagne is for the effete on foreign shores.

The chores are never completely done,
and the wax-candles melt in the heat.

The taxes are intolerable, and the injustices too much to bear,
as we lean upon the crutches that support us through history.

A DEFINING MOMENT FOR AMERICA

The blackberry patches, scooped-up news of home,
on the muddy fronts, sending out correspondences,
privately revealing the hurt beyond the musket-balls.

The young soldiers, North and South, closing their eyes
on a true conflict long enough to swap coffee & tobacco,
as Lincoln captained war's first cause: to preserve Union.

The events of Fredericksburg, then Chancellorsville,
uncontrollable costs of life, men paying their respects
by building shallow graves for their adopted brothers.

Lincoln solemnly following his inner voice
to hold fast to the need for military victory
and the necessary evil of Grant's butchery.

The sermons coming out of the North:
abolitionists claiming intervening hands,
guiding the fight for the freedom of slaves.

Gettysburg: the turning-point of pitched battle,
an un-buried purpose, perhaps a higher calling, and
the Address to honor the nature of national sacrifice.

The generation of Lincoln and Douglass
urged equality from a fabric of leadership,
suited for Dr. King & civil rights a century later.

The Civil War, broadly fought for black & white Americans,
forging an identity still in need of updates and interventions.
A people, united behind an Ideal, capable of transforming us.

DOWNFALL

A chance to dance
on the head of a pin &
crowded-out happiness.

The fall from grace,
so unbecoming you.

A turtle stuck in the road.

A collection of images
in descent & stored-up
in the trunk of memory.

She talks to me in stuttered speech
& attempts to get out the message.

I am fluent in this language of loss.

BATTLEFIELDS

The shrapnel undiscovered
beneath the skin of memory.

The undetected wounds
fester below the surface.

To heal what needs to be treated.

An Achilles' heel of unsubstantiated regret.

To hope for peace
in a lifetime of war.

These haunted dreams
open to interpretation,

where monsters escape in the dark,

and skeletons remain to remind us.

Invisible demons, once indomitable,
no longer able to inflict harm on us,

or conquer vulnerable enemies,
without the ammunition of rage.

Old wounds, hidden from view, still scare us into silence.

HARD-TO-REACH PLACES

A purple-mark, drawn from the heart of discontent,
protesting the invasive procedures of our time at war.
To insert & withdraw, needles stuck in combat zones,
until they are removed, air-lifted under moonlit skies.

The hawks, picking through the remains of guilt,
can't stay the course, witnesses to fractured lives.
The body politic is up-in-arms, the total loss of Vietnam
& now Iraq: coffins coming home on wide-screen TV.

We get away for a weekend at the Cape,
trying to make sandcastles with the kids,
sheltered from the news of a soldier gone
and platoons everywhere awash in grief.

The wrong priorities over which to weep —
our concern about a few cuts and scrapes,
adults tied up in traffic and running late,
stressed-out for God knows what reason.

Comprehensive plans for a full pull-out
from the local prayer-soaked battlefields.
Only bombs strike with surgical precision,
blowing open the careful stitches of peace.

We hope in emergency rooms, ill-equipped
to revive the pulse of the wounded masses
whose public talks were engulfed in flames,
leaving behind the private sphere of corpses.

The burnt ashes of a collective consciousness:
under the influence of a grand idea of freedom,
like a guaranteed transplant that didn't take, and
hollow promises to victims too hard to swallow.

WRITING HOME

The battlefield is littered with vultured excesses, carcasses of hate,
that creep onto the front, unannounced, on a frost-bitten morning.

To ponder and then to pounce upon the open wound of a meaning,
crafted in the backrooms, where the cigar smoke chokes fresh air.

The track of a soldier is assumed to crawl through the croaking night,
as the coffee & tobacco stain the teeth of those who write out of need.

To stop the war that rages within, a hawk wagers on digesting his prey
in the intermissions, the momentary lapses, that supposedly define us.

The map of a lifetime must be created outside the physical realm:
a cradle is only as good as the hand that rocks it, far from the terror.

To grade the spousal allowances, flesh & bone, in the circle of faith,
where the youngster's space is knitted and spurred on, round & round.

The bloody spectacle is renounced for its opposing grace, men & women,
in the theaters that compromise the beating-heart of a thick or thin history.

To hinge everything you possess upon the mantle of a documented winter:
a parting-wish hopes to better our natures in an eternal struggle to survive.

A letter to those we love is always in the background of endangered minds
as we can't avoid the mortal threat, a threat that spits on grandiose claims.

We compose our efforts, no matter how imperfect, or how many the drafts,
in a final push to pacify warring impulses in the view of well-lit goodness.

WOUNDED

She took me on a tour of duty, forced drafts
where the wind whistled through corridors,
where she spied in him a pale likeness to
the man he should have become.

To disappear into the mist, a man
enlisted for another five years,
with the false echo of discipline,
where lilies of the valley co-exist

with damaged plants, casualties of an early frost.

She guides him through the garden,
with the occasional lady-slipper, and
the cherished fit of a fortunate charm.

She is not disturbed by the clover, taking over
with a will of its own, uncaptured enemy of the good.

Nuisances spread like gossip.

To negotiate a necessary truce with himself,
a desperate cease-fire, oaths are promised
in the rescue mission, on protected grounds.

Life-long veterans engaged, with proper oversight,
on multiple fronts terrorized by fragments of narrative.

The whole story never comes out &
the intermissions grow shorter,
in theaters where the public poses at posts of gratitude.

She shoulders the burden in her garden, refreshed,
like a lady-slipper, once a bargain, now priceless,
dancing even in the shadows of sadness.

EXPERIENCING TRAUMA

His vision is clouded: he boycotts the prettiness of a cottage,
well-acquainted with a steeple underneath the wrinkled sky.

The dimpled-gray outlook is presented in gold-frame relief,
as the painting portends the ugly bout with an angry Nature.

A weather system becomes structurally unstable, institutional repose,
and the panicked responses from a lay-away plan of an uncertain life.

The curtains are drawn; the trailer swept up in the storm:
a confluence of events, veterans too late to keep a secret.

You never were known for an isolated destiny, icicles of change,
as the tags on your chain slip off into the scrutiny of night.

The truth is hard to come by:
shards of debris, bystanders.

To be at war with the late beat of an old-school channel:
where rules were designed to adhere, bandaged comfort.

The wounds are too deep to be covered on the surface,
as they go under a precise knife in a bloodied world.

The decisions to patch it up, the calls to make it right:
small potatoes operate in the grand scheme of things.

To redeem that which appeared out of your hands:
the clear message to settle the frantic pace of living.

The anger will pass, the frivolous will be satisfied,
and you can count on a sentence becoming a story.

The sum of friendly-fire is incalculable.

DISTURBED

The Devil infiltrates the marshmallow sky:
bones scatter far from my window of scars.

I aggravate Mars through a telescopic skin:
skeletons are broken in the spirit of Freedom.

To fritter away tears which have streaked into the abyss,
the sobbing are stopped & frisked in the habit of suspicion.

The frustrated are stunned by inconvenient observations:
milk & honey are unavailable in a violent, yet frail, world.

I scout out the visions that unearth the walking dead:
a mild harmony becomes extinct, in the vortex of loss.

To scoff at the black-holes of untold experience,
lessons are planned, explored, and then discarded.

The gravity of the universal dilemma weighs me down:
shooting-stars are ordered in a daze of magnificent light.

RETREAT TO RISE

To be true to the self that hides in a cave,

the guards compensate themselves with sleep;
a hummingbird freely emerges through a crack.

The light, at first, is difficult to take.

They notice the uprising in foreign lands,
the red-shirted struggle to survive the night.

The findings are in: the bloodbath on the Sabbath,
as solitaire is played in games, cleansed of relevancy.

And yet the force of revelations is too much to bear:
to tear at a heart that looks away from rescue-dogs.

The pound is full; the ground is bare;
and even the graveyards dispense with caring.

What can be done?

The human impulse is to ignore the suspicions of wrong-doing,
withdraw into a cave, and engage in an unaffected slumber.

The hummingbird, with an instinct toward flight,
foreshadows a light upon the olive-branch.

The dark is standing still, at attention & anxious,
like a soldier hoping to forget what he has seen.

The conflict is stressed: the best-kept secrets hide
behind boulders still in the path of hazardous duty.

Believers are forced into hand-to-hand combat.

DAVID F. KIRK

IN THE MIDDLE OF TURMOIL

The afterlife is adjusted dramatically upwards:
rafters crafted with a calm cover of angel-dust.

You promised the doves that they would matter,
so far from a past fattened with insurgent blood.

You speak of courage among a cast of forked tongues,
as the breaking news is leaked and work is suspended.

The streets pulse at the invigorated present:
rigorous attempts to relay what is wrong.

You have been so long asleep under a harvest moon,
as the weapons have been cropped out of the picture.

You are within reach of the proverbial top:
all sizes of dissent are seized in His name.

The customary assignments of blame, provocations,
and the preoccupation cannot be breached.

You listen to the latest version of the preacher,
who updates you on non-violent interventions.

You choose to bury your head in the sand, or
try to band together to reach a common end.

The harm cannot be undone &
the urgency cannot be halted.

You aspire to be like the mourning dove, having seen the worst,
but believing in the glory to greet those who put down their arms.

The seat of peace is not yet taken.

PROCEED WITH CAUTION

Tight-lipped disciples motion toward the red light:
disciplined followers tire of being in tip-top shape.

The gaping hole in the logic, and the stop signs of Reason,
upon a highway of a mind, adapting to lapses of judgment.

The turning point is concentrated in the aftermath of a wild ride,
as you pin-point guilt, confessions askew, as I have asked you.

The answers are tempted on a celibate Saturday night,
where you cast aside the sunrises that I share with you.

The fallible are forced off the road, in a gentle patter of rain,
as you soak in the flares of pain and the gathered repentance.

The gentleman and the scholar have skidded on the ramp of life,
with no way of getting rid of the accidents that face you & me.

To be reassigned to the spare-lemon mist, after high-risk adventures,
in which you have taken corners too quickly and tried to avoid contact.

An open inquiry is voided at the police checkpoint.

DAY IN, DAY OUT

The background noise is profoundly disturbing
as a weeping-willow bends toward its own end
and the gallows is the stage for a deep descent.

Wood is the instrument that plays for us —
the noted potential in the cradle of birth
& fixed paralysis in the coffin of death.

To step up to the challenge in the mills of thought,
where you proceed to lumber through dark moods
with a saw that cuts off the sharp edge of tragedy.

To claw your way back and to stay calm,
as the mind shifts to mid-level managers
ready and steady on a punched-in clock.

The hunch is that you are capable of a lift
after the shake-down of the coal stove and
the family of thoughts that give you a shot.

To revolve around a blue-suited Ideal,
where originality is held hostage and
you are the spitting-image of conformity.

The cookie-cutter Self that hid in the living-room is mourned,
like the dawn that lost its power to transform a blood-red sky.
To throw everything out in the open, including the kitchen-sink.

To kidnap a life for the express purpose of comfort,
the humdrum existence of a percussive soundtrack,
as you hear the refrain enough on the ledge of a song.

The wedge is driven routinely into a renegade heart.

RAINBOW-VISION

To twinkle in the frivolous sky, ambivalent about weighty matters,
with the Skittles scattered all over the dashboard, all over the seat.

The cash has been distributed to candy-rich investors, before prime-time,
before disputed tributes, where the Three Musketeers became irrelevant.

The television set is on, and Sponge Bob keeps coming back to mind:
life has been fun, like a never-ending cartoon with happy endings.

To wrap one's arms around the playful underworld,
even as the boys and girls out-grow silly episodes.

The imagined road to maturity is littered
with a hodgepodge of odd coincidences,

until the child, from the back of the station wagon,
reflects upon the passing of a priority-mail destiny.

To cram as much stuff as you can into a haphazard life:
the little stars hopefully get to their chosen destinations,

with the highs & lows registered in a utility vehicle,
transported through a universe, accustomed to icicles.

Your spirit, ever youthful, may freeze over, lightyears away.

PLAYING THROUGH

The notion of a family,
solid forms in a liquid world,
where you wait
for the cement
to harden again.

Again and again,
through miscarriages of justice,
through interruptions of illness,
both of which extend
beyond the endurable.

Until you have to endure it!

You play with firetrucks &
pretend to rescue people,
saving them from an emergency
they couldn't otherwise handle.

You play with dinosaurs &
pretend to rule the earth,
ignoring a real crisis
that wiped them out.

You play with Matchbox cars &
pretend to get into an accident,
glossing over the whiplash
that might hurt them for life.

You play & imagine best-case scenarios
in a desperately complicated world,
where the bottom drops out every day.

THE LIFE-PRESERVER

My affairs had been going quite well,
rather smoothly, like thin ice on a lake,
basking in the sun. Until a sinking
through crusted layers of instability.
In fact, I was issued a bitter shock.

It may have been better if
I had been wronged by another.
At least, I would have a party to blame,
a person to hold accountable.
Instead, I reach out to grasp — no one.

The questions well up like tears.
Is there any solace for imperial wounds?
Who will console the seemingly inconsolable?
Is there anything eternal but sorrow?
Will I be able to endure, like the blue spruce,
fortified against the cruelty of the coming winter?

The winter is upon me.

I am still, past frustrations, past illusions,
hanging on in a world of questionable truths.
I have lost my strength to complain
and am in the business of listening.
I hear your Word and am relieved.

My wishes, my sadness, my voice
seem to converge in my trust in you.
It is as if I am jumping into that lake in spring,
content to float, to wait, and to accept the waiting.
An eternity in the transcendent blue water,
immeasurable pools of grace.

HANGING ON

A man, at the mid-point of life, mysteriously adrift,
watches the fog roll in upon his well-crafted plans.

He stops to think & make his peace alone
in a rowboat on a lake in the mountains.

He smiles to himself. It is as if
the mountains anticipate his complaints
and say to him, "Why not you?"

Life is as it is — some paddle perpetually
against the currents, frustrated oarsmen,
while other passengers get a free ride.

His natural response is to curse the unfairness,
to reject the forces that threaten to pull him under.
He will not quit the fight to keep his head above water.

Over the edge of the boat, to the bottom of the lake,
he sees the muddied sediments & the mixed sentiments
that many feel in the underworld of sampled regret.

The private offer to persevere accepted,
he paddles home, with magical resolve
through the same fog we all may share.

The man may be out-of-work and unmarried,
still far from the shores of his expected bliss,
but he has committed himself to a bond with

the rest of the human enterprise and
the way it should carry out its affairs.

AN INSPIRED WAY OUT

I choose to live

like a sunflower,
bent with sorrow,

in a garden, overgrown with weeds —
dug up & then discarded, like regrets.

I hold out for Hope, seeing
a cultivated pattern, wildly possible.

Your kind words are transplanted &
nourished for poorly-rooted souls

while hawks patrol the neighborhood
& prey upon the half-asleep spirits.

Unawares.

Without you,
there would be no garden.

Without you,
there would be no growth.

The seasons note well the potential
for future blossoms, perennials.

I know, in this sacred space,
someone is still standing, or

kneeling in the aftermath of tears.

I have no choice but to live.

WITH FAIR WARNING

The beachfront trespasses rivet the antique soul.

New construction is all the rage &
I stop short with a permit for indestructibility.

Flagrant violations of code will not be tolerated.

The tight-lipped dream from the past:
sad dolphins fixed in shallow memory and
yellow rose petals floating in ankle-deep waters.

The official complaints are taken down by scribes,
who cannot shield us from the unexpected assaults and
shower of winds in an otherwise sun-drenched kingdom.

They never will be relieved of duty,
as they construct the translatable,
and save lost words, like lifeguards.

The line has been drawn in the sand:
I know the boundaries of what can be endured.

A soul, soon restored to excellent condition,
in a prime location, suitable for public access.

It tends toward a state of new normalcy, amidst
strange ruins rumored to be upon familiar shores.

The footprints erased; the shelter threatened;
and yet permanent markers finally affirmed.

I cannot deny it any longer: screened & boarded-up,
our hopes are suspended under the cover of a storm.

UNDER THE CIRCUMSTANCES

The twilight is beautiful this time of year: evaporated tears and
the instinct to build upon a platform from the mills of experience.

I hold out for better tomorrows with sparsely-decorated blessings,
even as we know gated-communities are located in other neighborhoods.

A mother and father create a mood in which anything is possible, and
I refuse to collapse under pressure from the weight of assisted living.

I push him gently down the ramp, always looking up, looking up
for the positive atmosphere we are trying so hard to construct.

We work with limited materials and minimal displays of grief
as we revisit the scene, with clean hands washed in good faith.

I may not know the outcome, or possess diamond-ring consolations,
but I still attempt to shine with the singular effort to make the best of it.

My current position is like the condition of a burning candle,
not operating with up-to-date wiring, but still offering a light.

I put off the threat of melting-down and appreciate what I now can see:
the bright side of a difficult life, refusing to be defined by a handicap.

The inspiration is written on the wall, structures of support,
and the acceptance of a thought that is not yet up-to-code.

I love you. I love you because there is nothing else I can do,
and all the metaphors & meanings cannot obstruct that view.

I try to use the treated-lumber of a well-designed past,
to expect something beyond a permanent slumber.

The sunset rivals the remote gathering of stars,
constantly on the lookout for a perfect ending.